JASON
REYNOLDS

GROUNDBREAKING STORYTELLER

JASON REYNOLDS

REYNOLDS

GROUNDBREAKING STORYTELLER

TY CHAPMAN

LERNER PUBLICATIONS ◆ MINNEAPOLIS

To all the young readers with a dream.
Chase it.
Don't let anyone tell you your voice doesn't matter.

Lerner Publications Company
An imprint of Lerner Publishing Group, Inc.
241 First Avenue North
Minneapolis, MN 55401 USA

For reading levels and more information, look up this title at www.lernerbooks.com.

Main body text set in Rotis Serif Std 55 Regular. Typeface provided by Adobe Systems.

Designer: Martha Kranes

Library of Congress Cataloging-in-Publication Data

Names: Chapman, Ty, author.
Title: Jason Reynolds : groundbreaking storyteller / Ty Chapman.
Description: Minneapolis : Lerner Publications , 2024. | Series: Gateway biographies | Includes bibliographical references and index. | Audience: Ages 9-14 | Audience: Grades 4-6 | Summary: "Jason Reynolds's interest in hip-hop and poetry turned into a successful writing career. Learn about the *New York Times* best-selling author who has received a Newbery Honor, an NAACP Image Award, and many other accolades"– Provided by publisher.
Identifiers: LCCN 2023021717 (print) | LCCN 2023021718 (ebook) | ISBN 9798765610459 (library binding) | ISBN 9798765623831 (paperback) | ISBN 9798765614747 (epub)
Subjects: LCSH: Reynolds, Jason–Juvenile literature. | African American authors–21st century–Biography–Juvenile literature. | Children's stories–Authorship–Juvenile literature. | LCGFT: Biographies.
Classification: LCC PS3618.E9753 Z57 2024 (print) | LCC PS3618.E9753 (ebook) | DDC 813/.6 [B]–dc23

LC record available at https://lccn.loc.gov/2023021717
LC ebook record available at https://lccn.loc.gov/2023021718

Manufactured in the United States of America
1-1009630-51718-8/15/2023

TABLE OF CONTENTS

Jason Reynolds speaks after being named the National Ambassador for Young People's Literature in 2020.

On January 16, 2020, a crowd of librarians and young people cheered for award-winning writer Jason Reynolds. Reynolds stepped onto the stage at the Library of Congress's Coolidge Auditorium in Washington, DC. Librarian of Congress Carla Hayden presented Reynolds with a silver medal. She carefully pulled the medal over Reynolds's long dreadlocks. It shined on his chest as he stood at the podium. It was official. Reynolds had just become the seventh National Ambassador for Young People's Literature.

The ambassador's job is to help young people become lifelong readers. They also help children with education. As a writer of nineteen children's books, Reynolds had spent a lot of time visiting and talking with young readers. He was more than ready for the new position.

Reynolds spoke into the microphone about what an honor it was for him to be the ambassador. He also knew it was a responsibility and not just an award.

Library of Congress

The Library of Congress (*below*), the national library of the US, is the largest library in the world. It was created in 1800. It is filled with millions of books, films, recordings, photographs, maps, and other print material. In 2020 the library's collection exceeded 170 million items. It supports readers through such programs as the National Ambassador for Young People's Literature.

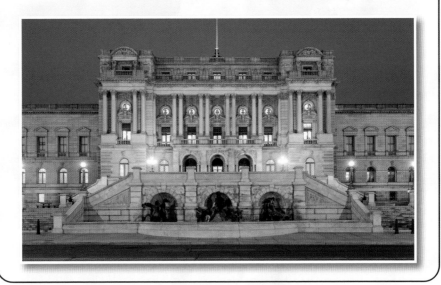

"It's a role, it's a responsibility," Reynolds said. "I'm going to do my very best to make sure that I uphold it and make something of it."

He also talked about visiting schools and how he let kids ask him anything. He told a story about a visit where a girl asked him to rap. Instead, he asked her to rap. She was nervous, but then she spoke into the microphone. She heard herself and lit up. The girl rapped in front of Reynolds and her classmates. This was an important moment for Reynolds. It showed him that young people need to have their voices heard.

After he had finished addressing the crowd, Reynolds sat with Hayden in red armchairs separated by a side table with two glasses of water and a pitcher. Hayden asked him about his life and plans for his new job. Reynolds said that he was going to visit schools in small

Carla Hayden and Reynolds talk and laugh during his ceremony to become the new ambassador.

Reynolds places his hand on his chest as the crowd claps for him.

towns across the US. Reynolds knew that not every child in the US had access to spaces for reading and expressing themselves. He planned to travel to these kids and create a space for them.

"My job is to let you say, is to give you the microphone and say, 'Yo, I'm 15, and these are the things that I care about,'" Reynolds said. "'This is what I'm concerned about in our world.'"

Reynolds wanted to be sure that all kids had the chance to share their stories and have their turn at the microphone.

Jacqueline Woodson

Jacqueline Woodson (*below*) is the author of over forty books for young people, including National Book Award–winner *Brown Girl Dreaming.* She was inspired by such writers as Nikki Giovanni and Maya Angelou.

Woodson was the National Ambassador for Young People's Literature from 2018 to 2019. Part of her job was deciding who would take over the role. She chose Reynolds and said, "I couldn't think of anyone else." She also introduced Reynolds when he took over the ambassador role.

It was estimated that in 1985, only eighteen out of twenty-five hundred children's books were written by Black authors. Woodson published her first book in 1990 and was one of the first authors to write modern stories about Black children. Woodson paved the way for many Black authors, including Reynolds.

Jason grew up in Oxon Hill, Maryland.

Finding the Right Words

Jason was born on December 6, 1983, in Washington, DC. His parents, Isabell and Allen Reynolds, raised him and his two older half siblings in Oxon Hill, Maryland. Every morning, Allen Reynolds got his children ready for school. Then he studied to earn his doctorate in psychology, the study of the human mind. While he was busy studying, Isabell Reynolds was working very hard to raise Jason and his siblings. She made sure they knew right from wrong and how to work hard for the life they wanted. Jason often says he gets his work ethic from his mother.

As a young Black boy, Jason had a hard time finding books he could relate to. So he didn't read books cover to cover. But music inspired him. Jason spent a lot of time listening to rap songs. He would take the pamphlets out of cassette tape cases, reading the lyrics to his favorite songs and being inspired by their poetry. Cassette tapes stored recorded music and were popular in the 1970s and 1980s. The pamphlets had the lyrics for each song on them. His favorite rapper was Queen Latifah. He loved her lyrics and related to the stories she told.

Years later, Reynolds said, "I always tell people the rappers of that time period were the [young adult] authors for us. They were telling our stories."

Rap lyrics helped Jason start writing poetry at the age of nine. They taught him to express himself through writing.

Jason used writing to help him understand what was happening in his life. When he was ten years old, his grandma died. Filled with sadness and a need to share his feelings, as well as comfort his mother, Jason wrote a poem about his grandma. His mother had the poem printed on the back of the funeral program. This was his first printed poem. Jason continued writing poems for the funerals of his great aunts and uncles. His poems provided comfort to his family and helped him process his emotions. Jason also discovered he loved writing and sharing poems.

That year Jason learned his parents were getting a divorce. It was hard for Jason to go through it and understand it. After the divorce, he didn't see his father much. He remarried and started another family.

Queen Latifah

Queen Latifah is a Grammy Award–winning rapper and singer. She was inspired by soul, reggae, and dance genres. Queen Latifah created songs that celebrated women. She began releasing music in the late 1980s. Back then, most rappers were men. With her powerful and poetic songs, Queen Latifah inspired women to become rappers. She also inspired Jason, whose passion for reading and poetry began with rap music.

Queen Latifah attends an event in 2023.

With everything going on, Jason had a hard time focusing on schoolwork. He liked to spend most of his time playing video games and basketball. But even though he wasn't completely focused on reading or homework, his love of poetry and music stayed strong.

When he was twelve, Jason started attending Bishop McNamara High School in Forestville, Maryland. He loved writing, but he didn't think his classmates thought poetry was cool. So he kept his passion a secret and only wrote when he was at home.

Jason's tenth-grade English teacher was Ms. Blaufuss. At first, Jason didn't like her. But by the end of the year, she was one of his favorite teachers. Jason enjoyed

This elementary school is next to Bishop McNamara High School.

Ms. Blaufuss so much that he later named a character after her in his *Miles Morales* book. She had encouraged him to take a small creative writing class at the school. In the class, Jason learned about different types of poems.

In 2000 Jason began to read his poetry at school assemblies. People loved his poems. He was surprised because he thought his classmates didn't think poetry was cool. He started to write his first poetry collection, *Let Me Speak*.

Jason was sixteen when he graduated from high school in 2000. In the fall, he started attending the University of Maryland. Jason made a name for himself there by reading his work at a Black Student Union talent show.

Jason attended the University of Maryland from 2000 to 2005.

Jason worked at Karibu Books for one year.

People were impressed with his talent, and he tied for first place. Another student, Delonte, brought Jason to a slam poetry performance, or poetry competition, where Jason read some of his work.

"I read my poem to basically nobody, but it was the first time I felt like I had a place. Like there was an actual space where I could come to work it out. And there were people just like me working it out as well," Jason said. "It changed my life forever."

When Jason was seventeen, he worked at a bookstore that focused on selling books by Black authors. At the store, Jason found Richard Wright's book, *Black Boy*. The book follows Wright's life as he grows up as a Black man in the South in the 1920s. It talks about difficult

Rap Is Poetry

Many types of rap music are enjoyed around the world. This music has different beats and sounds. In the 1970s, Black musicians created rap in the Bronx, a neighborhood in New York City. Rap combines poetry, slang, and musical sounds. Some of the beats were inspired by the blues, funk, gospel, and reggae. Rap is poetry set to a beat. Black musicians used poetry to speak out against racism and tell Black stories. Many of these stories weren't covered by other types of media such as TV and books.

Many people love modern rap. But this wasn't so when it was created. It has become a celebrated art form with people winning awards for their raps.

Jay-Z is an award-winning rapper, and he has talked about its importance. "Rap is poetry. . . . [If] you take those lyrics, and you pull them away from the music; and you put them up on the wall somewhere, and someone had to look at them, they'd say this is genius."

Even though Jason didn't read a book from cover to cover until he was seventeen, he had been taking in language, art, and *genius* from a very young age.

experiences that Jason related to. It was the first time he read about a character who looked like him and lived in neighborhoods like his. *Black Boy* was the first full book Jason read. It helped Jason realize his love of reading. He was amazed by Wright's work. Most books Jason tried to read took a very long time for anything exciting to happen. So he was surprised that by the second page of *Black Boy*, a house had burned down.

"I realized that I didn't actually hate to read," Jason said about Wright's book.

Richard Wright wrote novels, short stories, poetry, and nonfiction.

After he finished reading *Black Boy*, Jason started working his way through other classic books by Black authors. In his time working at the bookstore, Jason read everything from James Baldwin to Toni Morrison.

In college, Jason continued writing poetry and performing spoken word. His passion for writing only grew stronger as he got older. But this didn't mean he

In 2000 Jason read poems at an open mic night and saw Reheem DeVaughn, who would become a singer-songwriter.

Street Fiction

Street fiction tells stories that aren't real and often talks about characters in large cities. The books often discuss oppression, violence, and community. Street fiction is also called urban fiction or street lit.

Black writers created street fiction in the early 1960s. It became popular about thirty years later. But some people didn't think kids should be reading books that cover difficult topics. Others say that street fiction covers topics that many kids experience. Without street fiction, some kids wouldn't have stories that they can relate to. Several of Reynolds's books are street fiction.

got good grades in English classes. Jason failed a college English class the first time he took it. After retaking the course, Jason nearly failed again but earned a D, allowing him to move on and take different classes.

In one of those later classes, Jason met a professor he really respected. He asked the professor to look at the poems he was working on. The professor told him his poems weren't very good. It was a rejection that might've been enough to make most people give up on their dreams completely. But Jason didn't. For him, this rejection was familiar. He later said, "I've been told what I can't do my whole life." Jason kept writing poetry and stories, as he worked to become a better writer.

The Path to Publishing

In 2005 Reynolds graduated from the University of Maryland with a degree in English. He moved from Maryland to New York with his college friend Jason Griffin, a talented illustrator. Their plan was to publish a book together, with Reynolds and Griffin both writing the words, and Griffin adding beautiful paintings to the book. After a lot of hard work, they signed a book deal with the large publishing house HarperCollins. They titled the book, *My Name Is Jason. Mine Too.* The book was an autobiography about both men, their friendship, and how they'd moved to New York to chase their dreams.

When Griffin and Reynolds published the book in 2009, it didn't sell many copies and didn't make the publisher much money. Their strongest supporters in New York and Maryland weren't even able to find the book in stores. Reynolds's life didn't change overnight as he hoped it would.

Reynolds was living out of his car. And publishing his first book, something he had dreamed about for years, wasn't going well. To make things worse, Reynolds had applied three times to graduate school programs for creative writing. He thought these programs would help him become a better writer. But each time Reynolds applied, he was told no. The schools said his college grades weren't good enough to be accepted into their programs. So Reynolds worked at several jobs while he improved his writing.

Ain't Burned All the Bright

Griffin and Reynolds worked together on another book many years later. In 2022 they published another book of poetry and drawings, *Ain't Burned All the Bright*. It talked about everything from Reynolds losing his father to current events. Reynolds's poem is spread out over three hundred pages and is divided into about ten long sentences. The sentences are broken into tiny pieces on each page. Griffin's illustrations were first created in a pocket-sized notebook. The book quickly became a number one *New York Times* bestseller.

Jason Reynolds and Jason Griffin attend the *Ain't Burned All the Bright* book art party in 2022.

After years of trying to prove himself as a writer and being told that his writing wasn't good enough, Reynolds felt as though maybe he should quit. But even though he sometimes felt this way, he never gave up. The path was harder than he thought it would be, but he kept going.

Reynolds left New York, moving back to the familiarity of Washington, DC. He returned in 2008—the middle of the Great Recession (2007–2009). The US economy was struggling. Like many others at the time, Reynolds had a hard time finding a job. When he was offered a job stocking shelves at a department store, he took it. He made about $100 a week (about $141 in 2023 money). Unhappy with his work, Reynolds reached out to his father for help finding a different job.

Reynolds worked at Lord & Taylor in 2008.

Allen Reynolds was in charge of a mental health clinic in Maryland. He helped get his son a job there as a caseworker. That meant he helped people get the care and services they needed. Reynolds worked with twenty-seven people. Some of his clients had mental illnesses. Others had drug addictions or Tourette's syndrome. It helped him understand the complexities of people, which helped him with making characters. He learned to find the good in others, even if they'd made mistakes in their lives. But the job was difficult. Reynolds was so stressed that he lost 50 pounds (23 kg). He eventually quit his job. He moved back to New York to work at a clothing store.

At the store, Reynolds learned how to balance his job and writing. When the clothing store wasn't busy, he worked on a new book. The manuscript focused on a Black boy named Ali who finds himself in a fight because of a misunderstanding. Writing the book by hand, Reynolds kept working on it during his time at the shop. Eventually, the book became *When I Was the Greatest*. It was published in 2014.

This book was easier for Reynolds's fans to find, and it sold many more copies than his first book. Many readers loved his new book. *When I Was the Greatest* won Reynolds his first book award. In 2015 he took home the Coretta Scott King–John Steptoe Award for New Talent. The award is specifically for newer writers who create extraordinary work. After years of hard work and rejection, Reynolds's life was changing. It was beginning to look how he had imagined it. By working hard and staying focused on writing, he was able to quit working at the clothing store. This meant he could turn his attention to writing and traveling to meet with young readers full-time.

In the same year he won his first award, Reynolds published two novels. His first was called *The Boy in the Black Suit*. The 272-page novel follows a seventeen-year-old boy named Matt, who wears a black suit every day for his job at a funeral home. Matt learns to cope with the loss of his mother, and a father who makes many mistakes. The second book Reynolds released in 2015 was *All American Boys*. He wrote the book with young adult author Brendan Kiely. *All American Boys* follows Rashad Butler and Quinn Collins, both sons of soldiers. Together, the boys do their best to deal with racism and police brutality in their community.

The Rhythm of Words

From picture books to novels, Reynolds writes many kinds of books. But they all have a rhythm to their words. In the short film *Dear, Dreamer: A Portrait of Jason Reynolds*, Reynolds is seen tapping his fingers on the corner of his desk. He drums out the rhythm of his words, choosing the perfect ones to make his poems sound like a song.

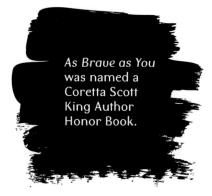

As Brave as You was named a Coretta Scott King Author Honor Book.

Both books were well received and sold well, but that didn't mean Reynolds kicked his feet up and relaxed. In 2016 he published *As Brave as You*. It follows an eleven-year-old Black boy named Genie and his thirteen-year-old brother, Ernie. Early in the novel, the pair are sent to spend the summer at their grandparents' house. Because their father and grandfather don't get along, the boys haven't spent much time with their grandparents. Throughout the summer, the boys get to know their grandparents, make new friends, and learn more about their family's history and losses.

In 2017 Reynolds's novel *Long Way Down* came out. It follows fifteen-year-old Will after his brother was murdered. Will takes the elevator in his apartment building to the first floor. He plans to kill the person who killed his brother. But at each floor, Will is visited

Reynolds talks about *Long Way Down* in 2017.

by a ghost of someone he knew that died because of gun violence. Will has to decide if he will hurt someone through gun violence or move on with his life.

Long Way Down was written as a novel in verse. It was told in poetry instead of sentences and paragraphs. Readers loved Reynolds's poetic and powerful language. Critics liked it too. *Long Way Down* was named one of the best young adult books in 2017 by *Entertainment Weekly*, Vulture, and BuzzFeed. It also earned awards such as the John Newbery Medal. The Newbery is given to an author that has had a big impact on books for kids.

Fans loved Reynolds's books, and they were selling well. Someone reached out to Reynolds about writing a book about the Marvel superhero Spider-Man. Reynolds agreed to do the project and wrote the novel *Miles Morales: Spider-Man*. It follows Miles, a Black and Latino

Reynolds during a 2017 interview

teenager who loves poetry. Miles is trying to escape his family's criminal past and become a superhero. Millions of readers loved the interesting and action-packed story. Reynolds also used the book to talk about complicated topics such as oppression and family.

The book did well, and Reynolds wrote a sequel to it called *Miles Morales Suspended: A Spider-Man Novel.* While the first book was written in prose, the second book was a novel in verse. The second book follows Miles as he serves an in-school suspension the day after he saved the world. He is sitting in the school when suddenly he must fight someone who could destroy the world's history, especially Black people's and other people of color's history. Miles has to fight for the past and present.

Reynolds discusses *Look Both Ways: A Tale Told in Ten Blocks* in 2019.

In 2019 he published *Look Both Ways: A Tale Told in Ten Blocks*. The book was a National Book Award finalist and followed the lives of ten middle schoolers, with each chapter following a different character's life.

Track Series

Reynolds's Track series is made of four novels about four different kids on the same track team. Each character has their own book, and they tell their story.

Ghost is the first book in Reynolds's Track series. The 2016 novel follows a seventh-grade basketball player,

Castle "Ghost" Cranshaw. He is a talented runner and sometimes has a hard time controlling his anger. Castle ends up running track for an Olympic-level coach. But Castle has a history of getting into trouble. To stay on the team, he will have to get along with his teammates and stay out of trouble.

The second book, *Patina*, follows Patina (Patty) Jones. Patty has to deal with her father's death and her mother's diabetes. Throughout the book, Patty must learn to juggle

Reynolds (*right*) speaks with another writer about his book *Ghost* in 2016.

all her responsibilities with being a good teammate and runner.

Sunny is the third book in the series. It follows a homeschooled thirteen-year-old, Sunny Lancaster. He only runs track to make his dad happy. Sunny learns to focus on his own happiness instead of his dad's.

The final book in the series, *Lu*, is about Lucas (Lu) Richardson. Lu is a young Black boy with albinism, a medical condition where a person has little to no melanin. Melanin is the brown and black coloring people have in their hair, skin, and eyes. People of color have more melanin than white people. Albinism often appears as white or light skin and hair. Albinism can affect people of all races. Lu is Black but has very light skin. People bully him for how he looks. Lu also learns that his parents are having another child, and he is worried about being a big brother. With the help of his coach, team, and family, Lu learns how to be a brother.

Reynolds's Track series tells the characters' stories and focuses on how the kids come together as a team. Readers also learn more about the team's strict but kind coach.

Passing the Mic

After Reynolds became the National Ambassador for Young People's Literature in 2020, he didn't spend much time celebrating. Just as his mother raised him to do, he got down to business. He began visiting different schools

Over one hundred thousand US schools closed during March 2020.

in rural communities throughout the US, as he had promised. He shared his story with young people across the nation and listened to their stories. He made sure the students he visited got a chance to hear their own voices. It was important to him that young people understood how powerful their voices are.

COVID-19 was spreading around the world. In March 2020, businesses and schools across the US closed to stop the spread of the sickness. Reynolds couldn't physically visit schools anymore to meet with students. Many classes were held online through video calls. Reynolds decided to meet with students that way. He knew kids had needed him before schools closed, and that didn't change after the closures. Some kids were having a hard time not seeing their friends. Others' loved ones were out of work because of COVID-19, and some had lost loved ones to the disease. Reynolds wanted to be there to help kids through it.

Throughout the pandemic, he went on three virtual tours to meet with students. He met with thousands of kids through video calls. Across the country, he empowered students to use their voices and share their stories.

In October 2020, Reynolds released a new version of *Long Way Down*. The new version was a graphic novel illustrated by Danica Novgorodoff. Graphic novels are told through images and writing. Some of Reynolds's writing was edited to fit the graphic novel. *Long Way Down: The Graphic Novel* was loved by longtime fans of the story as well as new readers. That year he also published *Stamped: Racism, Antiracism, and You.* A collaboration with Ibram X. Kendi, the nonfiction book explores racism in America,

Ibram X. Kendi is an author and historian who studies race.

Reynolds teaches students how to write books for young people at Lesley University.

as well as how to be anti-racist as a young person.

In 2021 he published *Stuntboy, in the Meantime*, with Raúl the Third providing illustrations. The illustration-filled novel follows a young Black boy named Portico as he copes with bullying and his parents' arguing. He attempts to save his parents' marriage and his neighborhood.

With his new book out, Reynolds kept up with being an ambassador. He even created a video series for students called "Write. Right. Rite." In the series, Reynolds engages viewers with writing prompts and creative activities. He wanted the videos to help kids learn how to tell their stories, express themselves, and play. The videos were posted to the Library of Congress website, where they will remain for young people to watch.

Reynolds was supposed to serve two years as the National Ambassador for Young People's Literature. But the Library of Congress was happy with his work, and he had inspired so many kids. So the program decided to have him serve another year. It was the first time that an ambassador's term had been extended. With COVID-19 vaccines available, Reynolds was able to return to doing what he originally promised. He traveled across the country and visited young people at rural schools.

In his school visits, Reynolds held conversations with students and answered their many questions. He let the students ask him anything. Many people who visit schools talk *to* students. Reynolds did something different. He talked *with* students. He listened to them, asked them questions, and answered theirs.

Reynolds's time as an ambassador ended in 2022. In the role, he traveled to twenty-five states, forty-seven schools, presented to over sixteen thousand students, and shared his love for storytelling. Back at the Library of Congress, a celebration marked the end of Reynolds's time as the ambassador. This time, his dreadlocks were partially tied back. Instead of a medal shining on his chest, his gold chains shined bright.

The New Ambassador

On January 24, 2023, Meg Medina (*below*) was inaugurated as the eighth National Ambassador for Young People's Literature. Medina is a Cuban American and an award-winning author. She writes picture books and novels for young adults. She is best known for her award-winning middle grade novels. During her ceremony, Reynolds talked about how Medina would be a great ambassador. He spoke to the crowd briefly before speaking directly to Medina, saying, "It's my honor to be here to celebrate with you."

Reynolds speaks with students in 2023.

This time, Reynolds was not introduced at length by Woodson and the Librarian of Congress. Instead, just as in his school visits during the ambassadorship tour, Reynolds was joined by two teenaged student ambassadors. Reynolds was open to answering any and all questions. As one of the students asked the first question, Reynolds remembered he was supposed to be wearing his medal that was awarded to him at the beginning of his ambassadorship. Pulling the shiny silver medal from his pocket, he unfurled the neatly folded cord and pulled it over his head.

He joked, "I feel like [since] it's my last day, I should at least put it on."

The student ambassadors asked him questions about his creative process, his passions, collaboration, becoming a full-time writer, and even general life advice. On the subject of becoming a full-time writer, Reynolds shared many helpful thoughts. He said, "If you love it, lean into it. Whatever that looks like for you. . . . But if you love it, if you love writing, you lean into it, and lean into it with everything you have, and have faith in the process. And if you do that every day, you'd be surprised the kind of space it'll make for you when you're 18, 19, 20, 21."

In the speech, Reynolds talked about how important it is for young people to find and use their voices. "You are your own ambassador. It's my job to just create a space for you to do so—all over this country. That won't stop when this is over, by the way," he said.

Afterward, Reynolds sat in the audience. The Library of Congress surprised him with a five-minute slideshow with video clips of some of the kids he had visited over the past three years. They thanked him for visiting and talked about how much his visit meant to them.

Reynolds's role as the National Ambassador for Young People's Literature has ended, but he continues working to improve kids' lives. He writes books that kids feel excited to read. In 2023 he released his first picture book called *There Was a Party for Langston*. It celebrates the writer Langston Hughes. Hughes wrote poetry, novels, short stories, and plays. His work focused on Black people and their lives in the 1920s to the 1960s.

Reynolds plans to keep writing books for young readers.

Reynolds's work continues to reflect the experiences of young Black kids. When he travels to talk with young people, he listens to them and their stories. He encourages them to keep trying their best, even when it is difficult. Growing up, Reynolds learned how to express himself through writing. But he didn't think he could make it a career. He kept going as people told him no again and again. He became a celebrated and award-winning writer.

Even when things were hard and he felt like giving up, Reynolds never did. He didn't give up when his professor told him his poems weren't very good, and he didn't give up when his first book wasn't an immediate success. If he had, the award-winning author would've never written the exciting books that countless readers love. He wouldn't have become the National Ambassador for Young People's Literature, and he might not have been able to change the lives of so many young people across the nation and world.

IMPORTANT DATES

1983   Reynolds is born in Washington, DC.

2000   He graduates from Bishop McNamara High School.

2005   He graduates from the University of Maryland with a degree in English.

2009   Reynolds releases *My Name Is Jason. Mine Too* with Jason Griffin.

2014   Reynolds publishes *When I Was the Greatest*.

2016   Reynolds releases *Ghost* and *As Brave as You*.

2017	He publishes *Long Way Down* and *Miles Morales: Spider-Man*.
	Reynolds becomes the National Ambassador for Young People's Literature.
	He releases *Long Way Down: The Graphic Novel* and *Stamped: Racism, Antiracism, and You*.
2022	Reynolds finishes serving as National Ambassador for Young People's Literature.
2023	Reynolds publishes his first picture book, *There Was a Party for Langston*.

Source Notes

8   "Jason Reynolds: National Ambassador for Young People's Literature Inauguration," YouTube video, 33:40, posted by the Library of Congress, February 20, 2020, https://www.youtube.com /watch?v=ljVahOoO7l0&t=2972s&tab_channel=LibraryofCongress.

10 "Jason Reynolds," 48:06.

11 "Jason Reynolds," 31:09.

13 "Wisdom from YA Authors on Leaving Home: Jason Reynolds," NPR, August 7, 2016, https://www.npr.org/2016/08/07 /489061736/words-of-wisdom-from-young-adult-authors -jason-reynolds.

17 Amy Moeller, "Bestselling Novelist Jason Reynolds Remembers His First Open-Mic Night at a U Street Bar When He Was 16," *Washingtonian*, February 10, 2023, https://www.washingtonian .com/2023/02/10/bestselling-novelist-jason-reynolds-remembers -his-first-open-mic-night-at-a-u-street-bar-when-he-was-16/.

18 "JAY-Z 'Rap Is Poetry,'" YouTube video, 0:39, posted by rocawear, June 14, 2011, https://www.youtube.com/watch ?v=HXR-ohNo3Ao&tab_channel=rocawear.

19 Tom Inniss, "Jason Reynolds: 'It's Only by Showing Up That You Will See Improvement,'" *Voice*, September 24, 2019, https://www .voicemag.uk/feature/6180/jason-reynolds-it-s-only-by-showing -up-that-you-will-see-improvement.

21 Jordan Foster, "Jason Reynolds: From Kid Poet to Award-Winning Author," *Publishers Weekly*, April 17, 2017, https:// www.publishersweekly.com/pw/by-topic/childrens/childrens -authors/article/73381-jason-reynolds-from-kid-poet-to-award -winning-author.html.

37 "National Ambassador for Young People's Literature," YouTube video, 13:44, posted by Library of Congress, January 24, 2023, https://www.youtube.com/watch?v=qprF0mnX-4g.

38 "Closing Celebration for National Ambassador for Young People's Literature Jason Reynolds," YouTube video, 8:34, posted by Library of Congress, December 13, 2022, https://www.youtube .com/watch?v=e5HpGFmbCII.

39 "Closing Celebration," 35:54.

39 Iyana Jones, "Jason Reynolds Closes Out Term as National Ambassador," *Publishers Weekly*, December 15, 2022, https:// www.publishersweekly.com/pw/by-topic/childrens/childrens -authors/article/91142-jason-reynolds-closes-out-term-as -national-ambassador.html.

Selected Bibliography

Alam, Rumaan. "Who Jason Reynolds Writes His Bestsellers For." *New Yorker*, August 9, 2021. https://www.newyorker.com/magazine/2021/08/16/who-jason-reynolds-writes-his-best-sellers-for.

de León, Concepción. "Jason Reynolds Is on a Mission." *New York Times*, October 28, 2019. https://www.nytimes.com/2019/10/28/books/jason-reynolds-look-both-ways.html.

Foster, Jordan. "Jason Reynolds: From Kid Poet to Award-Winning Author." *Publishers Weekly*, April 17, 2017. https://www.publishersweekly.com/pw/by-topic/childrens/childrens-authors/article/73381-jason-reynolds-from-kid-poet-to-award-winning-author.html.

"Jason Reynolds." Britannica Kids. Accessed June 25, 2023. https://kids.britannica.com/students/article/Jason-Reynolds/630934#:~:text=Young%20People's%20Literature.-,Early%20Life%20and%20Education,the%20lyrics%20of%20Queen%20Latifah.

"Jason Reynolds, National Ambassador for Young People's Literature." Library of Congress. Accessed July 1, 2023. https://guides.loc.gov/jason-reynolds/introduction.

"Jason Reynolds Named Library of Congress' National Ambassador for Young People's Literature." CBS News, January 13, 2020. https://www.cbsnews.com/news/jason-reynolds-library-of-congress-national-ambassador-for-young-peoples-literature/?intcid=CNM-00-10abd1h.

LEARN MORE

Cherry-Paul, Sonja. *Stamped (for Kids): Racism, Antiracism, and You.* New York: Little, Brown, 2021.

Library of Congress: Jason Reynolds at the Library https://guides.loc.gov/jason-reynolds/about

Library of Congress: "Write. Right. Rite." Series https://guides.loc.gov/jason-reynolds/grab-the-mic/wrr

Smith, Elliott. *Black Achievements in Arts and Literature: Celebrating Gordon Parks, Amanda Gorman, and More.* Minneapolis: Lerner Publications, 2024.

Time for Kids: 8 Questions for Jason Reynolds https://www.timeforkids.com/g56/8-questions-for-jason-reynolds/

Van Oosbree, Ruthie. *Acrostic Poems.* Minneapolis: Big Buddy Books, 2023.

———. *Free Verse Poems.* Minneapolis: Big Buddy Books, 2023.

INDEX

PHOTO ACKNOWLEDGMENTS

Image credits: Roberto Ricciuti/Getty Images, p. 2; Library of Congress/Shawn Miller, p. 6; joe daniel price/agency/Getty Images, p. 8; Library of Congress, pp. 9, 10; Desiree Navarro/WireImage/Getty Images, p. 11; Andrei Medvedev/Shutterstock, p. 12; Axelle/Bauer-Griffin/FilmMagic/Getty Images, p. 14; Brian Stukes/Getty Images, p. 15; JoeStock/Alamy, p. 16; Kevin Clark/The Washington Post/Getty Images, p. 17; Hulton Archive/Getty Images, p. 19; Paras Griffin/Getty Images, p. 20; Monica Schipper/Getty Images for Simon & Schuster Childrens Publishing/Getty Images, p. 23; Kristoffer Tripplaar/Alamy, p. 24; Marvin Joseph/The Washington Post/Getty Images, p. 27; Desiree Navarro/WireImage/Getty Images, p. 28; Bill O'Leary/The Washington Post/Getty Images, pp. 29, 31; Gary Gershoff/Getty Images, pp. 30, 40; Creative Touch Imaging Ltd./NurPhoto/Getty Images, p. 33; AP Photo/Photographer, p. 34; Faina Gurevich/Alamy, p. 35; Shannon Finne/Getty Images, p. 37; flickr (CC BY 2.0), p. 38; Backgrounds: P-fotography/Shutterstock; oculo/Shutterstock; Rayyy/Shutterstock.

Cover: Desiree Navarro/Wire Image/Getty Images; Nella/Shutterstock.